THIS TROUBLED WORLD

THIS
TROUBLED WORLD

JOHN DRINKWATER

Essay Index Reprint Series

BOOKS FOR LIBRARIES PRESS, INC.
FREEPORT, NEW YORK

First Published 1933
Reprinted 1967

LIBRARY OF CONGRESS CATALOG NUMBER:
67-30207

PRINTED IN THE UNITED STATES OF AMERICA

TO

NICHOLAS MURRAY BUTLER

CONTENTS

MAN AND THE MACHINE

MAN AND THE MACHINE

Fifty seems a suitable age at which to do a little stock-taking about life. If a man by then has not fairly well-defined ideas about what it means to him, or if he has not had sufficient experience by which to test his ideas, he is never likely to do so. On the other hand, if he is lucky, the edge will not yet have worn off his capacity either for thinking or feeling, and he can hope for a time to come during which ideas and experience may be expanded and fortified. I am fifty; and I propose to examine, in a discursive way, the meaning that life has for me as I look back on it, and the hopes that it inspires as I look forward.

About 1900, when I was a young man of eighteen, a spectacular picture appeared in the London *Daily Mail*. It was of a motor car that had astonished the world by doing a hundred-mile non-stop run. The car was a high-pitched, shaky-looking affair, something like a mechanical giraffe, and the driver, wearing an almost intolerably smug expression, perched high above the front wheels, might clearly be precipitated on to the road in front of him at any moment. He might, indeed, have been an allegorical figure of the pride that goeth before a fall. And yet, allegorically speaking, there was no fall. Year

by year those ungainly contours gave way to ever
more and more impressive streamlines, and now we
have cars that not only can do a hundred miles without stopping, but can do it in something consider-
ably less than an hour.

Then, ten years or so later, when I was just under
thirty, I was standing with some friends one day on
the Malvern Hills, where, five hundred years before,
Piers Plowman had meditated on a society gravely
menaced, it seems, by upstart ways, when high over
the brow of the Herefordshire beacon in front of
us came an aeroplane, piloted by a French competi-
tor in a pioneer flight round England. It was hardly
to be believed, and yet there it was. I remember the
first time when, as I watched a man pass me on a
bicycle in the street, his legs suddenly stopped going round, and the bicycle still went on with his feet
on the pedals. I had never heard of such a thing as
a freewheel, and I thought I was suffering from hal-
lucinations. How much more fantastic was the sight
of this little man on his great wings up in the air.
And that is not more than twenty-five years ago.

I need not elaborate the point. By far the most
striking change that has taken place during the generation that has passed since I was a child is that
effected by what is known as mechanical progress.
To the exploits and the efficiency of the machine
there now appears to be no limit. Every day brings

forth some new marvel, until the continual fuss that is made about someone who has broken, or has even failed to break a record, or has thrown away a perfectly good life by uselessly breaking his neck, has become inexpressibly tedious.

During the past thirty years the conquest of the machine by man has advanced at an astonishing pace. Not long before this began, Samuel Butler of *Erewhon* had warned us that one of these days unless we were careful we should witness the conquest of man by the machine. His vision was regarded by all but a few disciples as fantastic, and most people still point to-day to the marvels of mechanical science as the outstanding achievement of our age. So consuming has this passion for the machine become, and so widely operative its effects, that in thirty years it has brought about a change in the external conditions of society more rapid and more violent than any other that has preceded it in history. The congestion, not only in our traffic, but in every department of life, has become so acute that it sometimes seems as though the organism will be unable to bear it much longer, and that there must be some immense physical catastrophe. In one of W. W. Jacobs's enchanting riverside yarns, the skipper of a small vessel is very testy when his engineer insists on interrupting him in his cabin. He asks what the devil it is, to be told, 'The biler is wore out; it may bust at any moment.' Do we not, under the pressure of this congestion, sometimes feel that the biler may bust at any moment? And the congestion is largely caused by machinery.

The abolition of the machine, whether anyone may desire it or not, is as clearly beyond the scope of possibility as, shall we say, the abolition of fermented liquor. But the abuse of the machine, I am convinced, is a far more dangerous menace to civilisation than the abuse of strong drink. In a wisely ordered state the machine would have great and beneficent uses. Nevertheless, Samuel Butler was right. The machine is an invaluable servant, but it can be a bad and even a terrible master. Signs are abundant that it is this already. The explanation is simple. I have discussed it at length elsewhere, but I will repeat it here in a few words.

One of the cardinal instincts of man is for mastery. In his higher types, man is willing to undergo any discipline, endure any fatigue, offer any devotion in order to achieve it. The artists, the scholars, the scientists, the statesmen—I do not mean hack politicians, but genuine statesmen—will spare themselves nothing in order to serve their art, their learning, their knowledge, their statecraft. And in this service is the finest kind of mastery. These men, each in his own vocation, are creators, and there is no joy equal to that of the supreme sense of mastery stimulated by creation. This, however, is a delight that can be known to relatively few men, and the great majority are left with this urgent hunger for mastery without this most fortunate means of satisfying it. If they cannot master the more majestic problems of the mind, still they must master something. And in our own age ever increasing facilities have been given to them for this end. The average man, if he can master nothing else, can master a machine. It may be, as I shall show, that in a stricter sense the machine is mastering him, but his immediate consciousness takes no account of this. The simplest instance that I can offer is the driving of a motor car. Now, any fool can drive a motor car. It is a manifest fact that a great many fools do drive motor cars. I drive one myself. It is a very strange thing, but as a young man I was employed by an insurance company to inspect machinery for the purpose of estimating fire risks. My reports must have been masterpieces of bluff, because I never could make head or tail of a machine. I have no mechanical sense whatever; where it should be, is a completely blind spot in my mind. If an electric bell in my house goes wrong I haven't an idea what to do about it, except to telephone the plumber. Nevertheless, I drive a motor car. I will go so far as to say that I drive it rather well. I do not understand a single thing about it. If one of those little

pipes or rods or taps misconducts itself, I can do
nothing but sit impotently at the roadside until some
efficient person in a uniform comes by. And yet,
when I am driving my motor car, I am conscious of
a very pleasing sense of mastery. It goes as I direct
it, it starts—usually—when I tell it to, and, generally
speaking, it stops only when I wish. I can make it
go faster or slower by the smallest regulation of my
foot, and I can guide it to a nicety through all sorts
of difficult places.

I enjoy doing this. But I do not deceive myself
that it denotes any unusual intelligence on my part.
All the time I am passing people in other motor
cars whom I suspect of having hardly any intelligence
at all. Nevertheless, they drive their cars as well as
I do mine. And they are all enjoying the satisfaction
of mastery. Many of them augment their satisfaction
by driving their cars extremely fast, so that they will
reach their destinations in an incredibly short space
of time. It is true that most of them have no idea
whatever of how to employ the time so saved when
they get there; they will mostly be reduced to the
expedient of merely getting on faster to their next
destination. But how exhilarating it all is—man in
control of the machine.

With an aeroplane it must be better still. To drive
a machine, not along the road, but through the air
—this must induce a tremendous sense of conquest.

An even greater thrill, and, I am convinced, with even less strain on the intelligence. I must confess that I have never been in an aeroplane, but I am sure that it is easier to drive one through boundless space than it is to drive a car through the streets of London or New York, where there isn't any space at all. And how rich and tempting are the rewards of this newer and yet easier mechanical mastery. Any morning a young woman may walk out of the office where she is doing nothing much to promote the intellectual welfare of mankind, get into the cockpit of an aeroplane, fly to some quite unattractive place about which she knows and wishes to know nothing, and overnight become the heroine of two or more continents. She will then address public dinners on the advance that the world will make in civilisation by becoming air-minded. All of which is merely being hot-air minded. She isn't really thinking about civilisation at all; she is intoxicated by her mastery of a machine. And a very agreeable intoxication it is.

Again, the aeroplane may have its legitimate uses, though whether they can in any case compensate for the ghastly possibilities of its abuse in war may well be questioned. There, however, the aeroplane is, and no doubt there are good purposes that it can serve. But let us not be so mistaken as to suppose that the popularity of aviation has anything to do with its part in making us more civilised, if it has any. It is due to the fact that it provides the excitement of mastery in a very high degree, without necessitating anything like a relative degree of intelligence.

I have always admired rare skill of any kind. I have a great respect for the men who are good at games, and all my life I have tried to emulate them. I am pleased to pay my money to see them perform. I also respect the man who enjoys his games without displaying any notable skill at all. But I am not asked to take any notice of him, and I refuse to make a fuss about somebody who has done something in or on or with a machine that I know very well could be done by nine simpletons out of ten after a month's training. If these paroxysms of misplaced public enthusiasm were all, no particular harm would be done. But they are symptomatic of a habit that is infesting the whole of our modern life, the habit of regarding the machine not as a means to an end but as an end in itself. The sense of mastery derived from making the machine work is frequently accompanied by complete indifference as to what it is working for. Even in the factories where the slaves of the machine function in a daylong monotony that is dreadful to contemplate, the situation is just saved by the consciousness, very dulled it is true and almost automatic, that they too are controlling great forces. Above them, grade by grade the machine masters ascend, up to the creative engineer himself. And over that vast field of activity hangs the miasma of false aims, of confusion between the instrument and its purpose.

Our mechanical age is bewitched by this barren virtuosity. A striking example may be found in the work of the cinema studios. Here is a great industry almost entirely enslaved by the machine that should be its servant. The expertness of the camera men, the electricians and the mechanics is wonderful to watch. No miracle of the machine, it seems, is beyond their sorcery. Over them is the director, the super-magician, making all these masteries his own. What a temptation is here, and how fatal it is, may be seen on eighty per cent of the picture-house screens. The intrinsic enjoyment of the machine in the studio is as great in the production of rubbish as in the production of fine work, and since rubbish is so much easier to come by, why worry? Indeed, under the constant spell of this seduction, what time or incentive is there to learn how to distinguish one from the other? This is the drag against which all the better intelligence of the moving-picture business has continually to exert itself. Until the studios find master machine men, from the producer down, who can see the difference between photographing a fine thing magnificently and photographing a contemptible thing magnificently, all the efforts of writers and actors towards improvement of the screen will be frustrated.

This, then, is one of the principal things that has happened in the external organisation of society during my lifetime; the worship of the machine not for what it does, not even for what it is, but for the easily acquired sense of mastery that it provides. The discovery of this satisfaction has undoubtedly led to the neglect of other pursuits. The young man who forty years ago spent his evenings playing the cornet or making rabbit hutches in the garden, now buys a second-hand sports model and an imitation crash helmet, and takes to the road with all the assurance of Kay Don or Gar Wood, gentlemen whom I long mistook for topographical features. The young man may be as well employed with his racing car as with his cornet; that is a matter of taste. But the nature of the attraction which the car has for him has entrenched machinery so securely as a domination in our modern life, that it is now an almost hopeless task to place it again in its proper sphere of service. Most people who take any active interest in their radio sets are much more delighted to hear bad music from a station that is difficult to get than good music from a station that is easy. It is a straw that shows which way the wind blows.

The facile acquisition of mastery through the machine has discouraged patient enquiry. Where satisfaction can be readily experienced without the pains of learning, learning will fall to a discount. We need not pretend that in the pre-mechanical age the general public devoted its leisure hours to the higher refinements of culture, but this new mechanical activity of the masses has a deeper influence upon society at large than the old diversions of the cornet and hutch-building. These were private, if not always sufficiently secluded pursuits, while the machine today is a public habit, an example continually thrust before our attention whether we choose to follow it or not. And its influence is reflected in many aspects of modern life that have themselves nothing to do with machinery. We may consider one of these, as representative of the remote and unexpected effects that a prevalent public habit may have.

During the past few years there has been a much admired fashion in what is called frank biography. This does not mean pornographic biography, but biography which, according to its advocates, looks truth in the face even though it does not shame the devil. It is alleged to be a reaction against the sentimental portraiture of an earlier age, and is characterised by a rooted distrust of any features that give its subjects a momentarily attractive appearance. To suggest that a man sometimes behaves decently for the simple reason that he has decent instincts is, we gather, to betray a psychological ineptitude that is very debili-

tating to the judgement. Personally, the sight of a
suitable figure on a pedestal has never offended me.
I have never supposed that an act of reverence im-
plied that its object was without blemish, and I find
this sort of homage bracing rather than enervating
to my spirit. However, I can understand the mood
in which pedestals are provoking, and I realise that
with some people it is a natural state of mind. Further than that, I am all for humanising the monu-
mental figure in biography, but I do not notice
conspicuous failure in this respect among the more
important biographers from James Boswell forward.
Let the new iconoclasts take their victims from
the pedestals by all means, and set them firmly on
mother earth. Let the features be accommodated
to nature, and the gait and gesture be loosened up.
But when the object of these salutary attentions is
further naturalised by a limp and a squint that hitherto had been wholly unsuspected, is not a new kind
of sentimentalism being indulged that is even less
defensible than the old? It is akin to the affectation
of candour that rejects happy endings in fiction and
the drama even when the tragic ending that it im-
poses is not for a moment sustained by the pressure
of the story. The sentimental tragic or frustrated
ending is a great deal stupider than the sentimental
happy ending, and in modern literature far commoner.

But the fashion of which I am speaking bears more closely upon my present purpose. Any creative writer of experience will tell you that it is far easier to make an impression with a villain than a hero, if I may use these crude but convenient terms. Virtue is always more difficult to delineate effectively than vice, and the good man as a protagonist is in every respect a more exacting problem than the scoundrel. The reason for this is that the positive or virtuous aspects of character are much more complicated than the negative or evil aspects, and therefore demand much more careful examination before any convincing presentation of them can be made. Any failure in conduct is, when placed before us, in itself immediately exciting in several ways. It may arouse our resentment, we may share the transgressor's fear of consequences, we may pity the victims, and beyond these considerations there may be an almost physical response to the event, as there is, for example, if we witness an assault in the street. It is, in fact, usually the offence itself rather than the character behind the offence that first arrests our attention. Let someone of whom we know nothing at all pick a pocket before our eyes, and our interest is held at once; but let him give a sixpence to a beggar or help a cripple to cross the street, and we take no notice. For these virtuous acts—assuming them to be that—are not arresting in themselves. In order to interest us they have to be related to the character that governs them, and that is a very subtle creative process. Shakespeare's great achievement in characters like Macbeth and Othello is not in the presentation of their tragic faults, but in the suggestion of the higher nature in these men of which the faults are a betrayal.

So that even when there are acknowledged defects in the figure that is to be drawn for us, the finer artist will still be at pains to show them as contrasts to the better parts of character. This is where he has to prove his mastery if at all. Any over-stressing of the defects, while it can be sure of making an impression, is an exposure of the artist's mind. He is choosing the easy instead of the exacting way, and evading his responsibilities. If he goes beyond this, and not only makes undue capital out of the defects of his subject, but in addition attributes apparently good actions to unworthy motives, he is violating his artistic integrity even more seriously. And, in my opinion, many practitioners in the fashionable school of biography do this. The same thing happens in criticism. Abuse is always easier and more directly effective than constructive praise. To expound the merits of a work in an entertaining manner is the most difficult task that criticism can propose to itself, and requires an altogether finer intelligence than censure, however honest it may be. A critic like

Mr. George Jean Nathan, highly gifted as he is, has wasted half his time in witless scolding that may make people jump but never makes them think.

This too common artistic practice in our time of exploiting what is really a spurious candour in order to score easily, is, I believe, directly associated with the mass mechanical habit of which I have spoken. The delicately cultured writers who have set the modern fashion that I have been discussing would shrink in contempt or distress from the suggestion that they have been in any way affected by contacts so vulgar. But they have. Insensibly they have caught the infection, and it has worked. Confronted on every hand by a habit of easy mastery, a habit which is no less contagious because they do not recognise it, they have been contaminated by it themselves. These men do not lack either industry, intelligence or vigour. What they lack is courage, the courage to take their readers by the severe and difficult ways to truth and to resist the snares of elegant notoriety.

Stopford Brooke, a very celebrated Victorian, wrote when he was an old man, in a letter to me when I was a young one: 'I like it [some essay], but then I am of the nineteenth century, and do not mind being delayed and quietly brought to the point.' Deliberation—that more than any other is the habit of mind that during my lifetime seems to have receded

further and further into a Victorian distance. Snap-
decisions have become more and more the custom, it
may be the necessity, of affairs. People have persuaded themselves, rightly or wrongly, that in a world
of convulsions and cataclysmic change long hori-
zons and historical perspectives no longer matter, if
indeed they are not a positive hindrance to compe-
tence. We, too, have had our gains. Our social conscience is in many respects alerter, and our attitude
towards what are commonly called morals tends to
grow less dishonest. But the sacrifice of deliberation
is a serious loss. A critic of some fugitive reputation
in England has recently published a book in which
he maintains that since Keats there had been no poet
of any consequence in that country, with the excep-
tion of Gerard Hopkins, until the appearance of
Mr. T. S. Eliot. It is easy to dismiss this as the folly
that it is, but it is more than that. It is indicative of
a mood that has become dangerously prevalent in
modern life. This critic is on the fringe, if not at the
centre, of a school that has considerable authority
among the young people of England, and, I may add,
of America. I have even seen warm approval of his
views expressed in a journal of high literary standing. Of course, he cannot influence balanced and
mature opinion, but the mere fact that he is not in-
continently laughed out of court by everybody is significant. What can be the state of a mind that arrives

at such conclusions? Must it not be stripped of all sense of proportion, of the power to see life at any moment not as an isolated phenomenon but as an organic part of a continuous whole? This may sound platitudinous, but in the face of statements such as this, and their acceptance even in a little measure, we are forced back on the reiteration of platitudes. Such a pronouncement signifies not progress but disintegration. If it represented any wide body of educated opinion, our intellectual state would be desperate. Fortunately it does not; but it is decidedly of a sort with a great deal of mass feeling that is not educated. In politics, in finance, in commerce, we have lost our grip on the reality that is conscious at once of the lessons of the past, the necessities of the present, and the claims of the future. Like that fog-bound critic of poetry, our modern body politic has lost itself in a fog of self-interest that for long has been illuminated by no light from beyond. We must, we are told, adapt our minds to the conditions of a new age. The experience of our fathers can teach us nothing, and if we can save the world from utter ruin, it is the most that our children can expect of us. A desperate hand-to-mouth doctrine of expediency has usurped the place of principle and instructed prudence.

The consequences of this pitiful surrender to unreason are manifest throughout the world to-day. It slew the young manhood of a whole generation, and now it threatens to starve mankind in the midst of plenty. And still the insensate cry goes on: Arm, arm—barricade yourselves against your neighbours—recognise human nature for what it is—trust nobody. If we don't stop it, that cry will destroy our civilisation yet.

Happily, the forces of reason are active still. Active, many of us believe in spite of all discouragement, with a certainty that they will prevail. And here the artists have as usual done well by their generation. Small coteries, such as the biographers who deprecate whitewash so warmly, and often it seems to me with so little occasion, and substitute tar and feathers in their own practice, have been deflected from wider purposes to little affectations of their own. But the majority of writers who have earned any considerable esteem in my time have earned it by a steady determination to see their own age and their experience of it in relation to the tradition that is their inheritance; to base their observations not only on what they see but also upon the lessons of past endeavour with its achievement and failure; and to test their beliefs and aspirations not merely by expediency, but by principle founded on the cumulative experience of history. It is not my purpose here to examine the merits of individual writers, but a short list of names will point my pres-

ent argument. Bernard Shaw, John Galsworthy,
H. G. Wells, Lascelles Abercrombie, Charles Mor-
gan, Ralph Hodgson; Edwin Arlington Robinson,
Sinclair Lewis, Theodore Dreiser, Robert Frost,
Vachel Lindsay, Eugene O'Neill. Here are a dozen
writers, six English and six American, characteristic
of the achievement of our time. Poets, dramatists,
novelists, some of world-wide popularity, some of
secluded though established renown, others of new
reputation, they represent between them the greatest possible variety of aim and method. There is
hardly any aspect of modern life that is not considered by one or another of them, no spiritual mood
that is not explored, no habit of mind that is not displayed. Every shade of reticence and volubility,
composure and indignation, affirmation and dis-
sent, gravity and levity, acceptance and denial, here
finds expression. These men are as wide asunder in
their thought and quality as members of the same
race could be. But they have one thing in common,
a refusal to be stampeded by the transient modes
and agitations of their time. Vitally in contact as
they are with all movements and adventures of their
own day, they have regarded them always through
minds profoundly aware of the continuity of life,
that is to say through minds that, probably assenting
to no formal doctrines and even antagonistic to
church government, are essentially religious. Splen-

didly conscious of their own powers, they have pre-
served the fundamental humility that is inseparable
from vision. They have scourged the follies of their
age, but they have not mistaken them for evidence
that man has lost his five wits altogether. They have
refused to be deceived by appearances. The panic-
stricken behaviour that daily improvises new pana-
ceas, professes new loyalties, and is reflected in the
machine-worship of which I have been speaking,
might convince a superficial observer that the spirit
and the mind of man really had suffered shipwreck
in our time. The popular press is, I suppose, a faith-
ful guide to the interests of a very large section of
the public, and if this is so a very large section of the
public must be weak in the head and have an insati-
able taste for the recitals of minor and major crime.
Anything that will give an immediate sensation is
eagerly welcomed by the editors and, presumably,
by the readers. Quick reactions are what is wanted.
It is no matter for wonder. The publicity-mongers
of the world deafen us to quieter appeals with their
hysterical and mostly inarticulate din, and in order
to catch our attention the journalists have to attack
our senses with sharp incisive blows that have im-
pact but precious little meaning.

The writers, such as I have named, have thrown all
their influence into the scale against this demoralisation. They have seen that the figure of the mod-

ern man presented by the sensational press is not really drawn from the life. This denotes more acumen than might be supposed, for while it is easy to deride and denounce the sensational press, it needs a very level head not to be influenced by it. Every morning and every evening its voices scream across the world, and while we may be proof against their persuasion we can hardly persuade ourselves that they don't mean anything at all. The whole teasing business can't, surely, be just a pretence and nothing else. If the public to the tune of tens of millions daily devours this unprincipled and utterly unstable sensationalism, it is hard not to infer that here is a reliable indication of public taste and character. I can only say that if it were so, then the state of the world, discouraging as in many respects it may be, would be far more hopeless than it is. If the tone of the popular press accurately reflects the mentality of its countless readers, then civilisation must indeed be a lost cause, and the sooner it blows itself to pieces the better. A civilisation so bereft of reason is not worth saving.

But civilisation is not a lost cause, and the writers, of whom I have given a representative list, have shown us a world of men and ideas that, while it excludes nothing of failure and evil and pain, is turning still securely on its axis. It is a world deeply troubled by folly and misgivings, but it is not a world given over to the gesticulations of idiocy. Character and principle, sorely tried though they be, have not been abandoned. Amidst the betrayal of ideals, the sacrifice of honour, and the pursuit of shams, faith and purpose have not wholly gone out of life. Undeceived by superficial appearances, the creative writers of our time have seen the mind of man, greatly perplexed, but not overthrown. The scatterbrain and fevered sensationalism that is so displeasing an aspect of our modern life has been rightly diagnosed by these men as an ugly local distemper, not as an incurable malady of the soul. The literature of this distracted generation is not serenely detached from the turbulence of its time. It often echoes, or even emphasises, the stress in which it has been conceived, but at least it is not the literature of a madhouse. In preserving its sanity in a world that seems often to be insane, in refusing to regard man as the disaster that he would be if the figure reflected in the popular press were a true one, literature has done handsomely by its obligations.

Strangely enough, the very press that has so much to answer for in specious misrepresentations of the truth has also been liberal in its encouragement of responsible writing. There has never been a more curious example of the right hand not knowing what the left hand doeth than the editorial practice of debauching the minds of readers on one page and illuminating them on another. The same issue that contains a summary of the day's news in terms of overwrought and ill-proportioned violence, will contain also a clear-sighted exposition of some profound problem of life by H. G. Wells or Nicholas Murray Butler. With an even odder inconsistency, the newspapers will not infrequently castigate in their own leading article the very sensationalism of which their news pages are such striking examples. There might seem to be a certain cynicism in this, but, if so, there is something else besides. It is an implicit admission that the pages of sensationalism after all do not satisfy the intellectual demands of the average reader. When the editor of a popular newspaper asks a distinguished writer to write a special article for him, he does not impose conditions. The writer is not requested to make any concessions to what by the evidence of the rest of the paper might appear to be the public taste. He is allowed to express his own views freely and with as much distinction as he can. It is a fact that much of the most constructive polemical writing in our time has appeared under the auspices of journals that elsewhere exemplify the state of mind against which it is in constant protest. The instruments of confusion are thus a principal means of spreading the light. The anomaly may astonish but it need not inflame us. It indicates, I am sure, a realisation that the appetite to which the

cruder sensationalism appeals is a symptom, as I
have said, not of an incurable malady of the soul but
of a local distemper. It may be that the appetite is
already growing jaded. In any case, as we read, if we
do read—and we probably do—those unsanctified
pages, we can reflect with some composure that they
are not really what they seem. They present a picture of a spiritual collapse in man that is absurdly
extravagant, and even the designers are beginning
to know it.

The event above all others by which public conduct in our time has to be tested is the war. So vital
still are the issues that it raised, that it is difficult for
us in middle age to realise that there is now no one
alive under thirty who fought in it, and no one
under twenty who has any material recollection of
it. Already a new generation is arriving at maturity
with only hearsay evidence of its horror. If they are
to be persuaded that the first duty of the world to-
day is the prevention of its recurrence, they must be
persuaded, not by experience, but by us. What are
we doing to persuade them? The men who fought
and died in 1914-1918 were told with the most solemn emphasis of authority that they were fighting
a war to end war. The pledge may have been given
without a due sense of its implications, but given it
was by every leader in the allied, indeed in the belligerent countries. It was the slogan used alike for

recruiting and for stiffening the purpose of the people. What has the world done to redeem that pledge? It is a question of the most searching gravity. I shall attempt to answer it.

IS IT PEACE?

IS IT PEACE?

I recently saw a profoundly impressive play called *Miracle at Verdun*, by an Austrian dramatist, Hans Chlumberg, who met with a tragic death during the rehearsals of the play in Germany. He had been a soldier in the war, and like thousands of others in all the armies had come out of it with a spirit of fierce antimilitarism. His play is a notable contribution to the literature of bitter disillusionment that has in these later years attracted so much attention. Frenchmen, Germans, Americans, Englishmen—soldiers of every country have written books inspired by a passionate hatred not of their enemies but of war. These books are of two distinct kinds. There are the books that in the light of stark experience strip the war itself of all its glamour, and the books that search the consequences of the war, finding there a shameful repudiation of the cause for which, by general consent, the war was fought.

The former kind, of which I suppose the German *All Quiet on the Western Front* is the most celebrated example, has provoked several replies, chiefly by very hearty warriors who stress the cheerful courage and spirit of comradeship that ennobled the life of the trenches. We can admire the intrepidity of these writers a good deal more than their intelligence. No one is so stupid as to dispute the obvious fact that war is conspicuously an occasion for the display of those qualities. The most savage books of the *All Quiet* type record the display with an almost unbearable poignancy. No words can fitly celebrate the heroic feats of action and endurance that everywhere in the battle areas were the daily reckoning for four years. Nobody fails to recognise the splendour of that story. But nobody capable of two logically consecutive thoughts can ever suppose that the splendour is in any sense a vindication of war, or makes a war a splendid thing in itself. Any kind of disaster is likely to be an occasion for heroism. A child trapped in a burning building will find a dozen or a hundred heroes in the crowd eager to risk or sacrifice their lives to save him. But I do not know that anyone would advance this as an argument for setting fire to houses that contain children.

The plain fact is that war is a senseless barbarism for which no justification is possible. Incidentally it engenders heroism; but it also engenders savagery in its most ruthless form. The agony of body and mind that it inflicts is past computation. It inflames the lust for killing in men naturally gentle, it defiles all beauty, and it levels the brain of man with the mud. War is man's confession of his abject failure to carry on his job with a decency that would do no more than set him above the brutes. It puts every ethical consideration out of court. Gilbert Murray, in his remarkable book *The Ordeal of This Generation,* tells a story for the truth of which his name is a sufficient guarantee. Some English troops at Christmas time found themselves entrenched within a few yards of the German line. There was a lull in the fighting, and the antagonists were making a pathetic little celebration of the season by exchanging small gifts—a pickled herring for a packet of cigarettes or so. Authority heard of this and disapproved of it as being subversive of discipline. The officer sent to stop it arrived at the moment when a young Englishman was about to throw a small pot of marmalade across to the German trench. This boy was ordered to throw a hand grenade instead. He threw it, and the horror of the act haunted him for years—if he is still alive it haunts him still. No terms can measure the biting tragedy of an incident like that—tragedy to everyone concerned—the commanding officer, his deputy, the wretched boy, the slain Germans who were making a little play with Santa Klaus. Anger with any one of them is misplaced. None of them was to blame. They were all the tragic victims of that bloody and maniac futility, war.

No: the glory of war is an argument that can convince nobody in his senses. There are advocates of its expediency. A very distinguished British scientist, Sir Arthur Keith, lately asked the students of Aberdeen University in a Rectorial address to regard war as a necessary means of keeping the earth's population in check—he called it Nature's pruning-hook. I ventured to write a short poem on the occasion:

Sir Arthur Keith of Scotland, there is judgement set between
Your Science and the Souls of certain boys in Aberdeen;
They took you for their Rector, and they asked you for your rule
That should be a thing remembered when they came no more to school.
And you told them that the Nature of your scientific ken
Made war a bloody pruning-hook to prune the earth of men.
Did you know, my Lord, that Nature has the nature that we seek,
Takes her bent, her cue, her bias, from the very word we speak?
You said this thing and, saying, you gave it fearful breath,
For each word for peace is life, and each word for war is death.
You bade your boys, Lord Rector, count this evil as a good,
And the bidding has engendered the evil in their blood.
If you have no better gospel for salvation of the young,
Then, in the name of Science, for God's sake hold your tongue.

Nothing that the soldiers have written in condemnation of war overstates the case. The case cannot be overstated. The worst that can be said of it is not bad enough. There are no considerations that can justify licensed murder as a means of settling disputes, even if it could ever be shown to settle them. And war never settles disputes. It cannot even claim that by bad means it achieves good ends. It achieves no good ends. Of what benefit to the world, or to any part or race of the world, has the war of 1914-1918 been? What the immediate necessity of this nation or that to engage in it may have been is a question to which a dozen answers will be given to the end of history. We are all of us sure, quite honestly, that our own particular answer is the right one. But, motives apart, what good has it done to anybody? What nation is there but has suffered by its incalculable losses in mind, body, and estate? War is not only rotten, it is inescapably futile. And I will go so far as to say that if we should be so mad and so wicked as to make war again, it will not matter in any moral conception of the world who wins it.

Miracle at Verdun is an eloquent example of that other type of war literature, of which bitter disillusion is the keynote. The story of the play is simple. The action takes place in 1939, on the twenty-fifth anniversary of the declaration of war. The French and German Ministers deliver orations in honour of the dead, and the rhetoric of each is aflame still with fierce national self-interest. At that moment, in the military graveyard at Verdun where French and Germans lie in common burial, the dead come to

life. In ghostly procession they go back among men
to learn what has happened since their sacrifice was
made. They find the old political feuds raging still,
the old national hatreds still burning, and no sign
at all of the promised new world that was to be fit
for heroes to live in. In an inarticulate agony of
despair they return to their graves. There are other
significant issues raised by the play, but that is its
governing motive.

The indictment is magnificently made in terms of
drama. The cynicism of the churches, the blind folly
of the statesmen, the personal rapacity of the people,
are exposed with a ruthlessness that frequently rises
to grandeur. Hypocrisy, greed, and antagonism are
everywhere still the ruling passions of the world.
Germany is nursing her revenge, France arrogant
in her new armed supremacy, America assessing the
catastrophe exclusively by the dollar standard, England drifting along in complacent self-esteem. The
churches, who disgraced themselves during the war
by becoming recruiting offices, are still stifling the
spirit in a cloud of material sophistries. Even the
solitary enthusiast for reform can hear nothing but
the demagogic ranting of his own voice. Altogether
it is a world mired in baseness.

We can hardly complain that the indictment, taken
literally clause by clause, is unjust. Nowhere, if we
are candid, can the accusation be met with denial.

Statesmen have been obscurantist, the church irreligious, and the people covetous. Folly and fear and avarice between them have conspired to throw the world into a state of panic that is dark with the threat of a new convulsion that might be even more terrible than that of 1914-1918. Pride still at every step impedes the way of conciliation. Hunger and wretchedness have what seems to be a stranglehold on great masses of the population. By millions of people the future is contemplated with dull despair from a present that compels them to live on a meagre charity, and robs them at once of responsibility and self-respect. Dreadful tales are circulated—they are repeated in *Miracle at Verdun*—of secret activity in the laboratories where gases to poison the air and bacilli to infect the reservoirs are being prepared for the next war. Fleets of aeroplanes are said to be in readiness to destroy the capitals of the world overnight. These reports may be inventions, but in any case they reflect thoughts that are in men's minds. Disregarding them, we still have plain evidence that all is very far from being right with the world. The pledges of the war have not been redeemed. Suspicion still muddies the clear channels of communication between the peoples, and nobody is satisfied with a settlement that settled nothing. Seeing what they saw, well might the resurrected dead go back to the oblivion of their grave at Verdun.

The real answer to Chlumberg, however, is that he did not allow them to see all. Doubtless, in the dark and bitter agony of his own soul, he was incapable of seeing all himself. It is impossible to see his play without being deeply moved by its passionate sincerity, and no one who believes in the theatre can fail to admire the art with which the passion is controlled. No play about the war has held my interest in a surer grip, and I have nothing but respect for the dramatist who wrote it. And yet I do not think it is a great play. It has penetration of an extraordinarily searching kind; but it has not vision in the larger sense. The indignation is tempered by severe self-discipline, even by humour, but it is not transfigured in the light of that justice which is the supreme mood of creation, whether it be comic or tragic in purpose. The spirit of Chlumberg burns in the play with a consuming intensity, but it does not shine upon the play from without in revelation. What *Miracle at Verdun* tells us is true, in the sense that none of it is false; but it is false in the sense that it is but a part of the truth violently isolated from its organic place in the whole. We cannot reproach Chlumberg for the violence. We can but pity the noble anguish of which the violence is a symptom. But we should rigorously examine the very powerful impression made by the play. We can learn much even from so stark a pessimism, especially when it

is handled with Chlumberg's firmness. The danger is
that we too may be possessed by the passion of this
partial truth to the exclusion of the larger reality
that contains it. As an antidote against easy opti-
mism, such a white heat of anger is wholesome. Nevertheless, passionate despair, although it may be
more admirable than bland satisfaction, is not less
open to the charge of sentimentalism. I have re-
ferred to the tragic ending in fiction that does not
persuade us of its necessity, and is even more tiresome than the manipulated happy ending. It is in
this that Chlumberg seems to me to fail, not the less
surely because it is negatively. His integrity is beyond question. The false endings of which I speak
are usually designed to create an effect of uncompromising honesty. Chlumberg's dreadful conclusion
is entirely innocent of any such desire. There is not
a pretentious moment in his play. And yet the fault
is there. Great tragedy presents always the failure of
something noble. *Miracle at Verdun,* with scarcely
a moment's relief, presents a world utterly ignoble,
not fallen from grace or with any promise of re-
demption, but base as it was in the beginning, is
now, and ever shall be. If Chlumberg's perception
of the world to-day be an accurate one, then there is
no man in it who is not either a fool or a scoundrel,
without a ray of reason to lighten his folly or a gen-
erous idea to leaven his corruption.

Clearly, this is not a sober statement of the facts.
Sobriety of statement was not Chlumberg's concern,
but it is necessary for us to return to it from the
splendid gloom of his intoxication. It is idle to pretend that there are not many dangerous influences at
work in the world to-day; but it is no less idle to pretend that no effort is being made to defeat them.
The League of Nations, that European germination
of an American idea, is the mark of much criticism.
No great constructive institution can fail to be that.
It is true that the efficacy of the League has not yet
been tested by any major crisis, and it is true also
that there is a risk of relying too confidently on an
authority that, aiming at no less than a reconstruction of world policy, has at present had but a dozen
years in which to formulate its principles and put
its machinery into working order. It would be no
matter for surprise if it took the League half a century to become the effective guardian of the world's
peace that many of us believe it is certainly des-
tined to be. But in the meantime the League is per-
forming a service of incalculable importance in
creating an atmosphere in which it becomes increas-
ingly difficult for any nation to kick over the traces,
if a metaphor may be retrieved from an era of locomotion that is now almost extinct. One of the main
obstacles to progress in this matter is that there are
a great many people whom you cannot persuade

that by preparing for a catastrophe you do not necessarily prevent it; that, indeed, you may quite possibly precipitate it. There is little doubt in my mind that the last war was directly attributable to the international temper that had been cultivated by the advocates in all countries of what were called, not without cynicism, ample defensive armaments. The people of each country were told by their leaders that they must be fully armed against the not improbable attacks of other countries. The argument is a dreadfully specious one, and many people who are not at all convinced by it are afraid to say so lest they should be considered unpatriotic. If an Englishman, for example, is asked whether he would be prepared, in order to set an example by disarming, to risk the violation of his homeland by another power, he needs great moral courage to say yes, he would. If he does, he will be freely accused of weak-minded idealism, if not of treason. But the plain fact is that armaments did not prevent the last war, and that the rumours of new armament in the world to-day are by far the most alarming symptoms of the imminent possibility of another war. It may be taken as axiomatic that if you have vast armaments and a standing army ready to use them, sooner or later they will be used.

It is, in my opinion, further axiomatic that if you talk war you will have war, and that if you talk peace

you will have peace. That is why the League of Nations, although it may not yet have proved its authority on any issue of capital gravity, is already an
extremely important influence for good, more important, perhaps, than is generally realised even by
its friends. It is a forum set conspicuously in sight
of the world from which the principle of peace is being continually emphasised. The effect of this must
be progressively powerful. From this assembly the
appointed representatives of the nations go back to
their peoples influenced by an environment in
which the contemplation of war is sternly discouraged, and the cumulative effect cannot but be far-
reaching. It is sometimes said derisively of the
League that it is no more than an organised, or un-
organised, talk-shop. The same thing is said of every
national parliament. A more imbecile objection it
would be impossible to conceive. Certainly, in any
democratic assembly a great deal of nonsense will
inevitably be talked, but even a council of sages
would not be constant in sagacity. The man who
tells you that Washington and Westminster and
Geneva are chambers not of wisdom but of hot air,
and that in any case what he wants are not words but
deeds, is usually merely advertising the fact that he
is himself incapable of the thought that words express. Words are the most potent of all instruments
in the management of the world. Setting aside their

supreme use in literature, no step forward has ever been made but by talking about it, and, it must be added, no step backward has ever been made but by talking about it either. Opinion is formed by the currency of words, and opinion governs the world. Every word spoken for righteousness brings righteousness to pass, and every word spoken for evil gives evil its opportunity in action. The individual responsibility of every citizen among us in this matter cannot be exaggerated. Loose talk even in private conversation about serious things does more damage than can be measured. We ought to be scrupulous about this. If I say in public, for example, that the ideal of abiding peace is not an impossible one, and then privately confide to a friend that after all, human nature being what it is, I fear that it can never be realised, I am being false to my own spirit. Faith in these matters must be absolute, or it is worthless. When Christ said that faith could remove mountains He was using a figure of speech, but only by way of teaching that faith could do things not less but more desirable than that. We may not want to remove mountains, but we do want peace, and if our faith in the possibility of peace is uncompromising we shall achieve it. The very existence of the League is an assertion by the peoples that they believe in the possibility, and I am firmly convinced that the world is under an obligation to do everything in its power to fortify that witness.

Speaking as I am to Americans, I should say that
I do not presume to think that America is dishonouring that obligation by its present abstinence
from official participation in the councils of the
League. In the same way I never thought that
America was culpable for not entering the war
sooner than she did. I believe that if America joined
the League of Nations the impetus given to the
peace movement throughout the world would be
enormous, but I am convinced that America alone
knows, and this not by expedient or material tests
but on grounds of public morality, when if ever she
ought to take that step. I have far too deep a faith
in the character and the destiny of the American
nation, and far too warm an affection for many
Americans, to believe for a moment that a narrow
doctrine of isolation has anything to do with the
present decision to keep away from Geneva. You
have hitherto thought that your influence for good
in the world can be exercised more usefully outside
the League than in it, and although we can none of
us be sure what history may think of the wisdom of
your choice, I am certain that history will not question its honesty. And in the meantime you are in
fact exercising a very powerful influence for good
outside the League.

It must be borne in mind that the League in itself is less than the opinion that it represents, and

through which it came into being. In turn it has become the clearing house or crystallisation of that opinion. In its present state of development, the League cannot be expected to be entirely secure in authority, and crises will arise, such as that brought about by the Japanese adventure in Manchuria, which may find it unprepared with an effective solution. But even if the League had at any time to undergo a radical reconstitution, it is impossible to believe, in view of what has happened since its inception in 1920, that it would be anything worse than that. The sentiment which is at once the origin and the solemn trust of the League has now, we may surely believe, too firm a hold on the world to suffer effacement through any mishap to its principal organisation. If the League, not yet grown to its full strength, should be unequal to some momentary strain and collapse, there would be an immediate and concerted movement to reëstablish its powers and influence in some other form. We need not anticipate such a contingency, but it is clearly not an impossible one. Our faith is that if it should arise it will not be fatal to a cause that in recent years has been so passionately advocated by the best minds in every country.

For that is one of the chief misrepresentations of Chlumberg's play—that no effort has been made to relieve the world of the fear that is paralysing its economic and spiritual life. Unwearying effort has been and is still being made. The work of many peace organisations is reflected in the tone of political leaders the world over. Briand, Brüning, Kellogg, Ramsay MacDonald, Hoover, Mussolini— all these men have spoken unequivocally for peace, and the words of these and a hundred others are set clearly on record. There are other voices, shrill and menacing, and the cause of peace has not yet been placed beyond jeopardy. Much, very much, remains to be done, but it is a travesty of the truth to say that nothing is being done. The general temper of the world to-day is unquestionably for peace. So earnestly is this so, that any nation wishing to break it would already feel, and be made to feel, that the breach would be regarded by the rest of the world as a crime. Cynicism on this matter is easy. We are told that the alleged moral influence of the League has no practical means of making itself effective. It is, in a measure, true. There is still a danger that one nation or another might suddenly run amok in a belligerent fit, and that the League as such would have no means of bringing it to its senses. Though in this connection it should be added that the Kellogg Pact, which although it is not actually an instrument of the League is an extension of League ideals, pledges the signatories, that is to say the civilised world, to the abnegation of war in terms so decisive that the moral guilt of any nation dishonouring the Pact could hardly escape general condemnation. Further, the one nation that has threatened to withdraw from the League, did so not in open defiance of League principles, but on the plea that the League itself was acting in defiance of them. This, naturally, may well be a political sophistry that any nation would employ in similar circumstances, but at least it indicates an anxiety not to be regarded by the world as setting the principles at naught. It is a negative acknowledgement that the principles are sound.

This is not merely a finespun interpretation of the facts. The sentiment of the world is favourable for peace, and in the face of all discouragement we must never slacken in our will to consolidate it. The continual kaleidoscopic shiftings of political power in nearly every country do not promote international order. We vaguely feel that in the general domestic confusion anybody's house might be broken into before it was realised what was happening. As this figure represents a fleet of aeroplanes that might poison a city in an hour, we cannot afford to neglect the risk, remote or not, for a moment. Incidentally, I have one suggestion to make. Disarmament in general is being seriously discussed, and we may have confidence that its advocates will not weary in well-doing. But there is one feature of disarmament

which has not yet received the specific attention
that it demands. I recently asked a very well-in-
formed authority whether there was any foundation
for the rumours of preparation on a large scale of
poison gases and even disease germs for use in war.
He is by no means an alarmist, and he replied that
while the rumours were probably exaggerated, he
was not at all convinced that they were without sub-
stance. He said that it was not irresponsible pessimism that viewed the possibility of one or more of
the capital cities being substantially destroyed by
these means within the next ten years. And he is a
man who, in high office, is devoting his life to the
cause of peace, and doing perhaps as much as any
man living to promote it. If, then, there is the smallest margin of doubt on this dreadful issue, a general
condemnation by the governments of such methods,
and even an undertaking not to employ them, is not
enough. The peoples of the earth should not rest
until, by whatever influence they can command,
they have made it imperative for every government
in the world to ascertain the places where this dev-
ilish work is being done, to publish their knowledge, and in the name of common humanity to
stamp them out as they would stamp out a nest of
gunmen. Any activity of this kind is as criminal as
murder on the highway, and the moral sense of the
world ought to rise in determination that it should

be outlawed. The scientist who is using his talents
and his knowledge for such ends is an antisocial
menace of the most contemptible kind, and should
be treated as such. Here is a campaign for the press
to undertake that would bring it everlasting honour.

I have, I think, made it clear that I am not blind
to the dangers that surround us. But we must not so
far fortify them as to let them destroy our courage.
To be aware of them is necessary, but it is necessary
also to keep our faith in the forces that are opposed
to them. To lose faith is treason—it is to comfort the
enemy. Chlumberg in the white heat of his indignation may be forgiven for his refusal to look
through his disillusion upon moderating truth; we
may even be grateful that such a passion here and
there should show us the situation as a spiritual ca-
lamity unrelieved by any gleam of hope. The very
fact that so brave an intelligence can be afflicted by
the circumstances in this way should intensify our
realisation of the tragic possibilities that surround
us, and brace our determination to neutralise them.
Let us salute Chlumberg, but let us not emulate
him.

Distance, I know, lends enchantment to the view,
even though it is but the enchantment of escape.
Constantly to us in Europe come words from America assuring us that you too know the dangers to be

your own. And the words are convincing. Nevertheless, it is no matter for surprise if you should sometimes feel that they are less immediate here than on the other side of the Atlantic. Paris, London, Rome, Berlin—any of these might fall overnight to an enemy that had gone mad, but hardly New York. Well, I don't think that is a safe bet, and it will become less so with every year that passes. If this kind of devilry is ever to become the normal technique of war, as, if wars go on, it certainly will, then there will be no place on earth beyond the reach of its devices. No; we are all in this together. Peace is against the interest of no nation; and there is no nation, whether it may be on what is called the winning or the losing side, that can hope to survive another war without demoralisation from which recovery might well take generations. No nation can ever hope to survive another war with honour, for by the Kellogg Pact the nations have undertaken, in the most solemn and binding terms, on no account to engage in war again. The Kellogg Pact at present has the authority of no executive or legal machinery. It makes no explicit provision for dealing with any subscribing power that repudiates the agreement to abolish war. It is merely the sworn word of practically every nation in the world never again to take up arms. The oath is a simple one; let us repeat it:

The High Contracting Parties solemnly declare, in the names of their respective peoples, that they condemn recourse to war for the solution of international controversies, and renounce it as an instrument of policy in their relations with one another. . . . . [They] agree that the settlement or solution of all disputes or conflicts, of whatever nature or of whatever origin they may be, which may arise among them, shall never be sought except by pacific means.

That is plain enough. The Pact was signed in Paris on August 27, 1928, by the United States, France, Belgium, Czechoslovakia, Great Britain, Germany, Italy, Japan and Poland. Other nations subsequently added their signatures. The parties to the Kellogg Pact declared themselves to be 'Deeply sensible of their solemn duty to promote the welfare of mankind.' If hereafter the pledge there given to the world should be broken by any one of them, we should indeed have to confess in humiliation that mankind was bankrupt of honour.

Let us assume that the contract is observed: that the consent of mankind has secured peace not only in our time but for our children, perhaps for our children's children. What, we may ask ourselves, is the world to make of its peace? Given peace, we need not greatly fear the other difficulties that confront us. Poverty after riches may be very unpleasant, but it is not disastrous. Revolution, provided only that it be bloodless, may cause us inconvenience, but it cannot hurt the foundations of our life. The violence that has attended the social change in Russia is not, as some alarmists appear to think, inseparable from revolution. I know people in England who regard left-wing Socialism as a menace of civic dissolution and bloodshed in the streets. I think that the fear is absurd. During the past thirty years a social revolution has been taking place, in England as elsewhere, far more basic in its effects than anything proposed even by the communist left wing of Socialism. But because it operates without external violence many people fail to realise that it is a revolution at all. It has sometimes imposed an unduly sudden economic strain on a small class of the people, but otherwise it has done harm to no one and good to the greater part of the community. The most striking manifestation of the improvement is to be seen in the young men and girls of what used to be called the working classes, chiefly I suppose because they were supposed to do nothing but work. The change is most noticeable in the girls. Upstanding, smartly dressed, frank and self-confident, they seem in their emancipation almost to be bred of a new race. Moralists who will slobber over any offence if only they are allowed to patronise the offender, but who cannot contain themselves when independence goes with conduct that does not conform to their pattern, see all sorts of lurking or palpable evils in the new freedom. There are dangers, but not comparable to those attending the old enslavement. Spirited people when it comes down to fundamentals are always more moral than spiritless, and the sooner the official moralists realise that the new age is going to take no notice of their bleatings the better for their own peace of mind.

The betterment that has been effected, even though it can express itself at present in no more intellectual form than cheap silk stockings, is symptomatic of definite social progress. It has been gradual and not convulsive, and so it has hardly been noticed by the people whom chiefly it benefits. The new proletariat is not externally conscious of its advantages over the old. But in the deeper consciousness which is life itself, just as breathing is life, there has been great gain among the masses in self-respect and initiative. People of mature taste and intelligence will often be shocked by the follies and pretensions of a half-educated democracy, but the wiser sort know that a venture like the education of democracy, so much sublimer in conception and so much more exacting in its demands than any ameliorative design in history, cannot be judged by the audit of a day or even of a generation. We must not, since we cannot, be in too great a hurry. Similarly, we must keep our heads about an issue so acutely immediate as that of unemployment. No one in his senses can be indifferent to the misery of mind and body that attends this economic spectre. The world is desperately striving to find a solution of this most urgent of problems, and there is no one among us who would not eagerly accept it if it could be found. But it will not, it cannot come suddenly. The origins of the malady were gradual, and the cure will be slow. The most important thing for us to realise in a long view of the situation is that the social conscience of mankind is awake to-day to these two paramount necessities—the fulfilment of a dem- ocratic educational ideal, and the redress of eco- nomic injustice. The difficulties would be enor- mous, even if the effort to these ends were being made with universal good-will; they are aggravated by bad-will, in part merely ignorant, in part delib- erate. But, if the world is left in peace, the difficul- ties can and will be overcome. Our control over natural resources of all kinds is such to-day, and the growth of a general instinct to use them for the pub- lic good is so marked, that one thing only can hinder us in our approach towards an era of material pros- perity and moral enfranchisement unparalleled in history. That one thing is war. Dismiss the fear of that, and there is nothing good for which it would be foolhardy to hope. We will, in the faith that our pacts are not shameless lies, dismiss it, and I pro- pose next to ask what our hope may be.

SPECULATION IN UTOPIA

SPECULATION IN UTOPIA

There is no period in history in which Utopian dreams have not been indulged by man. There have been men in every age who, despairing of the follies and abuses of their own time, have turned to the conception of an ideal state. It is certain that if any one of these Utopias could be realised, the ideal state would after all be found to be imperfect, and under its government men would turn again to fresh images of a regenerated world. The ideal of a state all justice, all equity, and all vision, is not likely, within any evolutionary period that our minds can apprehend, to become a reality on earth.

To concede so much, however, is by no means the same thing as saying that things have got to take their course, however evil it may be, and that it is no use trying to deflect them. The condition of our society may in many respects be bad, but it would be very much worse were it not for the constant determination on the part of a great many people to put the wrong right, and a fixed conviction that in a substantial measure it can be done. For instance, many of us to-day may realise that the state of our ideal conception is beyond the hope of achievement, and yet we may see in the single purpose of keeping the world from war an ideal worth the most passionate service that the Utopian temper can offer.

The Utopian sentiments which I now wish to submit for consideration may first be defined in a general way. I am not here concerned with the Utopia that I might imagine if I could remould this sorry scheme of things exactly to my heart's desire; if what I wanted I could effect merely by the waving of an enchanter's wand. The most lovely of modern Utopias is, to my mind, visualised in William Morris's *News from Nowhere,* but I do not propose to journey even to a world so strictly within the bounds of human reason if only we really could be reasonable. Morris, we will allow, asks too much for our present consideration.

Nor, on the other hand, can I correct my impressions by strict economic knowledge. I was educated—in a very rudimentary way—at the Oxford High School, and I have never been so proud of the fact as recently when I was reading Sir Arthur Salter's *Recovery.* For he and I were at the High School together, and to have been at school with the man who wrote that book is something to be proud of. A more masterly diagnosis of the sickness from which the world has been suffering since the war has not been made: I know of none so authoritative. Nor do I know of any righter, decenter counsel as to what the treatment of the malady should be. It is refreshing, in a degree that can be understood only by reading the book itself, to come upon a mind that sees the truth in the light of uncompromising realism and what must be almost unrivalled knowledge, and is yet high in courage at the end of its investigations. When a man with so terrible and so literal a vision of the dangers that beset us tells us that the ways of escape are not closed, we may well take heart. His approach to the problem is mainly along economic lines. He has many wise things to say on the tendencies and accidents of human nature, but it is the economic fabric of society that chiefly engages his attention. A more lucid guide through what to most of us must often seem a hopeless mess it would be impossible to find. And yet even Salter writes:

> Ever since the Industrial Revolution there have been recurrent periods of prosperity and impoverishment but in spite of the long, patient, skilled and organised enquiries over many years, in the U. S. A., in Great Britain, in Germany and elsewhere, the nature of the cycle is still imperfectly known. The most vital and most urgent of the problems set to the scientific economist by the practical necessities of man is still unsolved.

The writer himself goes a long way towards the elucidation that we seek, but I certainly cannot solve economic problems by which even he is perplexed.

I said earlier that faith was necessary to the establishment of peace. It is necessary also to the restoration of economic equilibrium. The basic recovery

from our witless economic confusion must be a natural process, the normally healthy will of man making for life in this as the will of the earth makes for
the life of seedtime and harvest. Salter points out in
closely reasoned pages that the old system of economic *laissez-faire* is being superseded in our time
by a new one of what he calls 'control and planning.'
The relation between money and industry became
dislocated, and functional disturbances took place
in the whole economic structure of which money
and industry are the chief constituents. The competitive system began to fail in the automatic ad-
justments by which the economic life of the world
had been regularised without central control or de-
liberate planning. Crash followed upon crash in
consequence, and men like Salter see recovery only
by some such control and planning as will substitute the principle of private effort for public good
for that of private effort for private good. I need
not point out that philosophically the difference is
an elusive one, but in practice we can see easily
enough what Salter and the others are at. The old
system assumed that if every man took care of himself the public good was logically assured. It now appears that as some men are much more capable of
looking after themselves than others, the theory
does not quite work out in practice, and it is proposed to exercise some central influence upon the

way in which the individual serves his own purpose, and relate it to a wider necessity. With economists of Salter's quality taking the matter in hand, we may be hopeful of the results. But they would be the first to see that basically the recovery must come through that naturally healthy will of man, making for life. Without this the economist can do no more than the husbandman without the natural will of the earth. That the will of man is to-day as favourably set for economic recovery as it is for the establishment of peace, there are many indications, plain to anyone who moves about among his fellow-creatures.

Let us assume, then, not with easy confidence but with courage and faith, that we are approaching a period when peace is secured and economic justice secured also. A necessary condition of these ends must be the removal from past contracts of clauses tending to perpetuate bitterness and hatred. I am not competent even to suggest what revisions should be made in the Peace Treaty, but that some revision should and must presently be made is clear. One extraordinary psychological blunder was made at Versailles. Far-sighted people must have seen what was happening, but no one seems to have been able to prevent it. There was in the spirit if not in the letter of the Treaty a blind assumption that its terms were to be carried out by the generation that made it. And already we are being faced by the fact that a new generation is at the point of maturity, for whom the Treaty is not an act of its own, but a legacy from a quarrel about which in any personal sense it knows nothing. The injuries, the passions, the jealousies, the fears and the suffering that were inflamed by the war and reflected in the Treaty are fast drifting away from living remembrance, but the Treaty still remains. Here is a danger that must be honestly met.

To consider the case of Germany alone. If we are to apportion blame for the outbreak of war in 1914, then the German militarist party must bear the principal share of it. Moreover, since the war Germany has, to put it modestly, been no more accommodating than other nations in the work of an enlightened reconstruction. Sentimental appeals to pity the poor German may well leave us cold when there is the much larger urgency to pity the poor World. But let us set all patriotic indignation and national prejudices aside, however well-founded they may be, and consider the facts.

Fourteen years after the termination of the war, Germany, with a population of seventy millions, is still effectively in the position of a culprit nation. To say that this is her own fault may be true, but it does not get us very far. It may be argued on moral grounds that it would never do to let the nations believe that they can commit any kind of outrage and escape full payment of the consequences. It would, I think, be difficult to maintain that attitude even if it could be shown that any one nation ever was or ever could be singly responsible for a world disaster such as that of the Great War. Even then the mitigations of time would assert themselves, and immediate events would take on new aspects when seen in historical perspective. But when the responsibility has, however wrongly, at no time been anything but a matter of fierce dispute, then the doctrine of prolonged national penance in the name of morality will be fiercely disputed also, and sooner or later, in the practical working of the world if not in the theoretic mind, it will have to be discarded. That is the point at which, whether we like it or not, and whether it is ethical or not, we now are in the German question.

The Germans, men and women, who are now thirty years old were children when the war ended; they took no part in it, and they had no word in its settlement. They are the flower of the country's young maturity, beginning to take over control of its work and policy and to shape its ambitions. These people, the millions of them, are industrious, highly intelligent, they cultivate physical fitness and they are very determined. It may be excusable for us in the high light of past events to tell them that they must be humble and contrite in their hearts, but the plain fact is that they will take no notice of us, they will not even know in their hearts what we are talking about. The point need not be laboured. Put a great body of young Americans or young Englishmen in the same position, and see what the answer will be.

The world has got to relinquish the idea that recovery from the material disaster of the war can be effected by one nation or group of nations in favour of the rest. The recovery can be made only by common consent and common effort. At the same time the question of moral guilt must now be removed from the sphere of practical policy and left to the academic historians. I do not suggest that Germany should now be given a free hand to do what she likes, but no country should be given that. International control of armaments, for example, is an imperative and immediate necessity, to be exercised, as we hope, over a rapidly diminishing scale in all countries. But it is folly to suppose that a great and virile nation, whatever its past misconduct may have been, will with the coming of a new generation accept penal disabilities, or that any good social purpose can be served by attempting to force it to do so. In considering our practical Utopia a third condition, then, has to be predicated in addition to those of peace and economic stability; we must, in the conduct of affairs, pass an act of oblivion, and see that every nation is allowed equal opportunity to benefit by the fruits of reconstruction.

One final word as to the peace and good-will that must be the foundation of any lasting recovery of the world's health. Although the Treaty of Versailles contained the seeds of many troubles, it has one presiding feature that makes it possible to reconsider particular defects by the authority of its own preamble. It was owing to the pertinacity of Woodrow Wilson that the Covenant of the League of Nations became the first Chapter of the Treaty, and the precaution upon which he then insisted was one of the wisest in the history of international affairs. The inclusion of the Covenant in the Treaty was strongly opposed at the Paris Peace Conference, and it was Woodrow Wilson who alone had the courage and vision to insist on this general assertion of the principles of peace as a preliminary to the discussion of particular terms. The incorporation of the League Covenant in the Treaty has in later years sometimes been an embarrassment to the League itself, but, as Arthur Salter reminds us, if Woodrow Wilson had not been inflexible against all opposition at the time, it is as certain as no odds that we should never have had a League of Nations at all. The Peace Treaty without the Covenant would have been the breeding-place of dispute that it still is, and it would have lacked the element that makes for conciliation and good-will. If the settlement had been made before the acceptance of the Covenant, the nations would inevitably have gone about their respective affairs intent each on its own interest only. To bring them back to conference in an international spirit would have been impossible. Woodrow Wilson, and he alone, saw that refusal to discuss any settlement at all until the Covenant was accepted was the only way of getting it accepted at all, and by that single act, if by no other, he assured himself of a memorable name in history. I suppose that even the warmest admirers of that great man allow that he had temperamental defects which to some extent impeded the conversion of his thought into political currency. The doctrine of accommodation that he advocated so earnestly to the nations he did not practice easily in his personal contacts. But when all is said, at a time when international morality was in grave danger of being repudiated altogether, he stood for basic principles with a moral tenacity that was displayed by no other statesman of the war. As a political tactician he lacked qualities which are conspicuous in many lesser men, but in stability and foresight his public character was, in my opinion, richer than that of any of his contemporaries.

Not only did the Covenant of the League introduce a wholesome general tone into the Peace

Treaty, it also made one specific provision that may at any time do the world great service. Had the Treaty stood without the Covenant, the initial steps towards any revision would have been exceedingly difficult. Even those people who realised that the terms of settlement contain active dangers to world peace might well say, 'Yes—but there the Treaty is, and who can interfere with it?' The Treaty itself now answers the question. Article 18 of the Covenant reads:

> The Assembly may from time to time advise the reconsideration by members of the League of treaties which have become inapplicable and the consideration of international conditions whose continuance might endanger the peace of the world.

The gate is wide open.

We of the war generation, that is to say everyone now living who is forty years of age or over, have between us made a pretty thorough mess of the social organism. We are laying upon the succeeding generation the task of correcting our errors, and the least we can do is to spare no effort to keep them from drifting into our own fatal follies. Already again there are millions of grown young people in the world who are quite ready to be seduced by the glamour of war, and it is our duty to warn them with all the emphasis we can that the glamour is a lying cheat, utterly divorced from a reality that is foul and demoralising. We who were adults in 1914 remember the heroic enthusiasm with which the nations mobilised for war, and we know the greater heroism with which through four years they bore the brunt of it. But we know also the futile waste and horror and degradation of it, and we have been learning ever since that it leaves nothing but bitterness and impoverishment in its train. Let us tell these newcomers that. Let us do what we can to set them mobilising for peace with an enthusiasm no less heroic. How infinitely more honourable, and indeed more heroic, would it be to defend the world by peace than to defend ourselves by war. Let us have nothing to do with the pretence that there are nobilities in man that war alone can exercise.

Civilized life itself under normal conditions [says Gilbert Murray in the book from which I have already quoted] provides the element of strife, effort and discipline, all the more effective because it is continuous and comparatively gentle in action, instead of being sudden and violent. . . . There is really a touch of something insane in the idea that civilisation or the general level of human character can best be saved and improved by war. . . . The apologists for war . . . get their minds badly confused because they continue to speak of war as if it were an element in human nature, like Strife or Fear or Ambition. They speak as if those who proposed to abolish war among civilised peoples were proposing to suppress the combative passions or eradicate one of the primitive instincts. . . . War . . . is not an instinct; it is a form of state action. It is not an element in human nature, it is part of a political programme. It is no more an instinct or an element in human nature, than the adoption of an income-tax, or state-owned railways, or a protective tariff on wheat.

Let us declare our failure to our children for what it is. Let us, in handing on to them an inheritance of social chaos, not be guilty of the even baser betrayal of allowing them to suppose that we have been through some glorious kind of adventure that is denied to them. Over the ruins that we call upon them to repair, let us at least erect a fiery cross.

Given peace in their time, and in what remains of ours, the world, as I have said, will regain its health. But in the new state we must be prepared for many changes, greater, perhaps, even than those which have taken place since the tide of democracy began to flow in full flood towards the end of the nineteenth century. As an Englishman, and I think I should say the same if I were an American, I find it difficult to draw instruction from the enigma of soviet Russia, but clearly we have to face the possibility that in the recovery of equilibrium the entire civilised world may, without a revolution of violence, adopt economic changes hardly less startling in character than those effected by the autocrats of Leningrad. I do not think that in this there is any cause for alarm. 'Change,' wrote an English poet, 'is the law of life on earth,' and, if we can but keep our heads and our tempers, we may very well approach change with confidence. Change conducted by peaceful means becomes healthy evolution, and we need not be panic-stricken by the plain fact that our economic system is now passing through a critically evolutionary stage. What we shall find when we come out on the other side no one can tell, but, given peace, it will be nothing to fear. It may inconvenience a few people, but it is likely rather to augment than to diminish the common good.

Certain specific results of the change we can foresee. At all times there are movements of the mass mind that, though they may be retarded, cannot be arrested. One of these in our own time is towards a more equitable distribution of wealth, and less exacting conditions of work for that class in the community which may roughly be described as wage-earners. The social will of the world has fixed itself on this end, and obstruction is futile. Legislation tend more and more in this direction, and, although it may be checked by brief reactionary moods, the issue may be said already to be settled. What shape the reform will take we cannot yet see, but there can no longer be any doubt as to its nature, nor can it fail to be salutary for the world. One particular danger attends it, which may be noted in passing. The work of the world falls, broadly speaking, into two categories. There is the work, engaging a minority of people, which is rewarding in itself; and there is the work, engaging the majority, which is rewarding only—or chiefly—by virtue of the wage that it earns. In other words, there are a few people who would go on with the work that they are doing even if they could afford not to, and a vast number who would drop it to-morrow if they could afford to. In an ideal Utopia all this would be altered. Disagreeable but necessary work would be shared equally by the community at large, while disagreeable and unnecessary work would be abolished. But I am not discussing an ideal Utopia. I am discussing the actual state towards which we now appear to be moving. In it there will remain a great majority of people doing work primarily for the wage. At some far distant date this may be remedied, but not yet. Already, however, the conditions of that work are being improved, and within a generation—always assuming peace—we shall find that the redress of legitimate grievances has been drastic. The masses may still be primarily wage-earners, but they will no longer be wage-slaves.

The danger of which I speak is that legislative reform may involve the minority which is engaged on work rewarding in itself. Increase of legislation, even where it is needed, is at best a necessary evil, and the wage-slaves themselves will be wise to watch that their new liberty does not entangle them too closely in fetters and restrictions of its own. There is a very prevalent type of mind that is as recklessly addicted to legislation as the drug-fiend to his dope, and the passion for ordering other people about is a far more serious social nuisance than a passion for cocaine. Democracy here must be very carefully on its guard. And particularly does the minority of which I speak, which includes the artists, the thinkers, the constructive and investigating workers of all kinds, need to resist any encroachments upon its freedom. Its work is of great value to the world, and can be done only by unfettered minds. Legislation is death to creative effort, and any attempt to regulate the light of the spirit will succeed only in quenching it. The harm, if any, that is done by occasional licence is not comparable to the harm that might be done by unintelligent supervision and censorship.

Another change that is inevitable is one of social convention. With the spread of education, the equalisation of opportunity, and the more even distribution of wealth, class distinctions as we have known them will disappear. The process is already in operation. There are few working-class families to-day some member of which has not advanced beyond the social status to which he was born, and the leaven is everywhere spreading. It is an error to think that in the new state there will be a general levelling of personal authority. But rank will not be what it was.

Intelligence, organising power, beauty, vision, and natural grace—these will, happily, be marks of distinction always. But they will not be the prerogatives of any class, and people who lack them will not be able to borrow reflected rank from those who have them because they happen to be born of the same stock. On the other hand, there will be no social detriment in work for which these fine endowments are not required. I can see a time coming when a highly intelligent President of the United States will not think it derogatory either to his gifts or his office to make his less fortunately equipped brother doorkeeper at the White House; doorkeeping, as he will rightly consider, being a very honourable occupation.

You may tell me that this question of class distinction has less reality here in America than in my own country. I do not find it to be so. It is true that your classes are more fluid in composition and less determined by inheritance than ours, but your social distinctions are as clear. When I visit an American house I do not usually find that my host asks his chauffeur and furnace-man to dine with me, and I notice that your more exclusive women's clubs are seldom frequented by the charming young ladies from the departmental stores. No; Mayfair and Madison alike, being civil decent gentlefolk, are very polite to servants, but it is quite clear always that they are being polite to servants. The new state will have servants still, but as in it everyone will recognise that he is a servant, while there will be honour done still to distinction, there will be no social condescensions, however well-bred. And that, in general behaviour, will be a clear gain.

The experts themselves, academic and practical, admit that they cannot foretell precisely the lines along which the economic reconstruction of society will take place, although men like Arthur Salter can expound clearly enough the direction in which we are moving. But one conclusion I think may safely be drawn. If the new system at present in course of evolution results, as it seems likely to do, in a more regulated production and more even distribution of goods and money, there will be an increased amount of leisure all round, and one of the principal problems of the coming age will be to learn how to employ it wisely. There must come a time when the mere achievements of speed will have lost their charm; when, in fact, people will begin to think not only of how quickly they can get to a place, but also of what they shall do when they get there. It may even be that rapid locomotion will be so commonplace an activity that it will entertain nobody, and that people, instead of thinking of how quickly they can get to a place will be more and more disposed to stay in the place where they already are. Since it now seems reasonably certain that within a few years a man will be able to sit in his office and talk at will face to face with anyone he chooses on the other side of the earth, rapid transit will become less and less a business necessity, or even advantage. It would not be surprising if we found that speed had already reached the zenith of its attractions and its uses. It will hardly serve to satisfy the leisure of the new age.

Sport and games will probably take an even more important place in the world than they do to-day. I say important advisedly. There can be no question as to their present popularity, but a great many people lament their increasing hold upon public attention. My own opinion, on the other hand, is that the widespread interest in such recreation is one of the most reassuring aspects of a sorely tried civilisation. I recently heard Jean Borota, that idyllic lawn-tennis player, warn his friends in an after-dinner speech against the dangers of giving sport an undue prominence in their lives. This from a sportsman of such classic achievement was a very gallant thing to say. Nothing is more tiresome than the man or woman who can think and talk in no other terms than those of sport, whether it be big-game hunting or contract bridge. No people are so dreary as those who make sport the most important thing in life, but there is dreariness too in the view that sport is not important at all. Apart from the fun of the game, and the usually wholesome excitement, it has this to recommend it, that on the whole people when they are engaged in it, or even when they are watching it, are quite naturally and simply being themselves. An interest in sport, whether as a performer or a spectator, may not be a very profound form of self-expression, but it is a genuine and eager one, and as such is valuable to the community. I have no sympathy with the people who complain of the crowds that in their hundreds of thousands every week pay a little money to see first-class football or cricket or baseball. For great numbers of these spectators the few hours so spent in release from drab and monotonous work are, perhaps, the healthiest of their lives. And even the people who are more fortunate in their work are all the better for the recreation. Professional players who receive a wage for entertaining us earn it very worthily. Their exploitation by shareholders is sometimes not so pleasing, but they themselves deserve the rewards that they enjoy. The leisure of the new state will certainly encourage yet wider developments of sport in all directions, and we should be unwise to regard it as a sign of deterioration in any sense.

A much more significant question remains, however. What place will the arts take in a peaceful and decently regulated state? Those of us who spend our lives in the service of one art or another may with some plausibility be accused of overrating the importance of art in the social scheme. Naturally we do not think that this is so, but the view is not altogether surprising in people whose contacts with art are casual. The material rewards that can come to the arts in these days are so great, that the desire to earn them by entertaining is often expressed in a somewhat pusillanimous disclaimer by the artists of any purpose to do more than entertain. Hearty showmen of the arts the world over are continually assuring the public that they are the said public's obliged and humble servants, anxious only to please, and that nothing is further from their accommodating minds than to enlighten or instruct. It is the cowardly betrayal of a great trust, and no spectacle is more abject than that of the artist turned opportunist. Of course every artist desires popularity, but no artist worth the name is prepared to achieve it on any but his own terms. Failure to secure recognition may mean discouragement to the artist, but compromise to secure it means death. Let the artists be honest and insist that their business is not to give the public what it thinks it wants, but what they, the artists themselves, think it ought to want.

I will put it boldly and say that the uncontaminated artist mind is the human mind at its best. The artist, while he is true to himself, has one fixed de-

termination—to express the truth as he sees it, and
that is the purest purpose to which the human mind
can be devoted. Expediency and art cannot breathe
the same atmosphere. The nature of the truth may
be pleasing or not to other people, but its fearless
expression is a deep enrichment to every other mind
that it reaches. I am never tired of repeating Shel-
ley's words of transcendent wisdom—'Poets are the
unacknowledged legislators of the world.' Never,
perhaps, has the nature of art been so decisively declared in a phrase. The influence of the integrity
that is art is incalculable. Music, painting, literature and drama—it is not too much to say that the
natural virtue in us owes the greater part of its
growth and education to these. Even illiteracy that
consciously pays little or no attention to the arts is
influenced by them far more profoundly than it
knows. It is a facile way of talking to say that a
world hard pressed in the satisfaction of its material
needs cannot afford to take art very seriously. The
decision long since in history has passed out of the
hands of people who speak so. Art is daily exercising its power with or without the consent of this
man or that. Even in times of stress and penury the
eternal verity remains that man cannot live by
bread alone, and in a world where the churches have
lost their spiritual authority because in one crisis
after another they have forsworn themselves, it has

remained with art to supply the nourishment by which also man must live. Many people realise this, but many more benefit by the sustenance without knowing whence it comes. The legislation of art is almost universal, but it is unacknowledged by the great majority of people because they have no external consciousness of it.

If the new state is to prosper, this conciousness will have to become more and ever more general. The influence that is indirectly felt will have to be intensified by direct experience. The lessons that are now learnt from art at second- or tenth-hand will be learnt from immediate contact with art itself. It is a hopeful sign that social reform is looking more and more to the coöperation of the artists. Community drama, community singing, folk dancing, these and other such activities are recognised as being something more than the agreeable amusements which indeed they are. People who talk impatiently about the education of democracy and complain that money used for this purpose is wasted, are very shortsighted. The new ideals of education are hardly yet a generation old, and half a century may well pass before their full effect is apparent. But that already they are exercising a deep influence on the life of the community there can be no doubt. I will not weary you with statistics, but the records of the public lending libraries in England during the past fifteen years are most illuminating. I cannot speak for other countries, but I have no doubt that the same state of affairs would be revealed. The increase in the number of books borrowed is remarkable, and even more so is the steady proportionate gain of the more serious forms of literature on the lighter. One note may be taken from the records. Among the novels lent out by a public library, a considerable number are works of importance, but the term fiction in general denotes the more superficial sort of reading. My novelist friends will forgive me for saying this, as their own books, I need not say, belong to the distinguished minority. In 1910 the free libraries in the county area of London issued to their readers 4,800,000 novels, and 1,600,000 works of general literature; a proportion of three to one. In 1930, twenty years later, they issued 10,000,000 novels, and 5,000,000 works of general literature, or a proportion of only two to one. These figures are more than mildly encouraging, they are of the highest possible importance if rightly considered in their relation to the future. People don't read serious books aimlessly. Nor, on the other hand, can they be driven into reading them. Serious reading is a symptom of a serious mind, determined to enlarge itself and to get a firmer hold on the problems of life.

And here, again, the process is subtler than we

might suppose. Generally speaking, people do not read serious literature for instruction, but for something much more valuable, enrichment of experience. Suppose an unlettered man should read a dozen of Shakespeare's plays, Pepys's *Diary*, Boswell's *Life of Johnson*, Emily Brontë's *Wuthering Heights*, Emerson's *Essays*, and Thomas Hardy's *Dynasts*. He would not thereafter be provided with a rule of thumb on the conduct of life, but he would bring to the conduct of life a mind altogether wiser and more competent than it had been before. No rational society can regard education of this sort as a pleasant indulgence for idler hours. It should be one of the first conditions of the community. As things are, we know that great material success often comes to men with wholly uneducated minds. They are not to be envied; they are, rather, to be pitied. They enjoy neither honour nor respect; they enjoy only the fawning of sychophants. Let such men lose their wealth, and where are they? Adrift, without resources or esteem. And if their success holds, how do they employ it? Without vision or personality, forced more often than not to leave the distribution of their surplus in the hands of other people who may or may not have the imagination that they themselves lack. There is no way in which the educated mind is not at an immeasurable advantage over the uneducated mind, both to itself and to the community. It is not rhetorical to say that an educated world would be a decent world, and nothing is going to educate the world so surely as habitual contact with the work of self-respecting artists.

The increasing leisure from wage-earning for which we may hope in these coming times should therefore be largely devoted to this most liberal form of education. Only so will people acquire the understanding, the poise, the sense of perspective and proportion, by which alone they can arrive at wise government of themselves and society. Activity that does not take the long view dissipates its energy, and the long view comes to us by education and in no other way. An enthusiastic young playgoer recently told me that he found the contemporary drama so exciting that he could not be bothered to pay any attention to the great dramatists of the past. I replied that without some knowledge of the old his knowledge of the new would remain imperfect, and that he would lose half his joy of it. Whether we realise it or not, we ourselves are inescapably part of tradition. Unless we know what the tradition is, we cannot know what our part is. And if we do not know what is being done by the best minds of our own age, we cannot perceive how most worthily that part may be fulfilled.

THE INDIVIDUAL SOUL

THE INDIVIDUAL SOUL

I have attempted to take a bird's-eye view of our civilisation as it is to-day, of its prospects in the coming age, and of our responsibilities to ourselves and to society. I propose now to discuss an obscurer subject, the nature and the hope of individual life in the midst of this vast communal strife and activity.

A rich and talented young man of twenty-six told me the other day that he found life enchanting, and that if at any time it ceased to be so he should not hesitate to put an end to it. He boasted that he was not afraid of death, although he asserted that he believed it to mean annihilation of his personality. He thought he was speaking candidly, but of course he wasn't. It is easy to say these things when the energy of life is in full and unfettered play, because they are said then without a real sense of their meaning. But no man actually contemplates annihilation without fear. Face to face with the possibility, we shrink from it. We should be more or less than human if it were otherwise. We desire immortality, in the generally accepted meaning of the word. What authority for the desire can we discover?

The formal authority most familiar to western civilisation since the time of Christ has been that proclaimed by the churches. To-day the churches or, to use the generic term, the church has lost touch with the active life and thought of the world. Doctrinal questions apart, it is no longer possible to respect an institution that even in our own lifetime failed mankind in the crises of both war and peace. The church in 1914 ought to have refused flatly to lend any support or countenance to the madness that was driving the world to defy every tenet of Christianity, and instead the church joined enthusiastically in the row to its lasting disgrace. There are, I know, thousands of priests within the church leading heroic lives of devotion and self-denial, but the church itself has lost its hold on spiritual reality.

Even the people who accept the theology of the church have been saddened by this failure. Those of us who do not accept it, and the plain fact to-day is that we constitute a majority, are not saddened but a little curious to know what will happen to a body that by its ethical failure must also weaken the doctrinal authority that we have always disputed. Before stating the grounds of this dispute, I may say that it has always been incredible to me that people should allow differences of faith to inflame personal antagonism; at least it would have been incredible had it not been for the dismal evidence that religion provokes more bad temper and malice than any other activity in the mind of man. Many of my best friends hold religious views entirely opposed to my own, but I should consider it a disgraceful thing if I were to allow the difference to diminish my personal regard or affection. And yet the record of religious controversy is the most shameful in the annals of history.

A book that recently attracted some attention in England is *Caliban in Grub Street,* by Ronald A. Knox, a priest with one of the most brilliant minds in the Roman Catholic church. Two or three of the leading newspapers had invited a number of lay contributors, including scientists, authors, business men, artists and doctors, to write on a variety of religious topics. *Caliban in Grub Street* is, in effect, a declaration that it is improper for such people to express views on matters reserved for the jurisdiction of the church. Here is the keynote:

I have never been able to persuade myself that, if this interest in religious affairs were genuine, it could fail to betray itself in increased church attendance; curiosity by itself, one would think, ought to bring men to church to find out what is being said there. [The naïveté of this, it should be remarked in passing, is below Father Knox's common form. He goes on:] I do not wish to assert that there is a positive decline of religious feeling; the hearts of our fellow men are not open to scrutiny. But I do entertain the uneasy feeling that the symptoms of our time are being widely misread. There is no evidence that people are more religious; there *is* evidence that people are fonder of talking about religion, and of talking about it in public.

It comes oddly from the representative of an institution which has talked about it incessantly for nineteen hundred years, a representative, it may be added, who talks about it at far greater length than any of the people about whom he is so severe in his book. I don't see what the objection to talking about it is, or that the privilege of talking about it should be monopolised by Father Knox and his ecclesiastical friends. It almost sounds as though the church had disputed Father Knox, on account of his ability as an advocate, to warn common laymen against meddling with forbidden topics—not to drive without a licence in fact. There was a time when the church forbade us to read the Bible, but it surely cannot be so simple as to suppose that at this time of day it can prevent us from talking about it.

Father Knox believes in revealed religion, the unique divinity of Christ, the virgin birth, the resurrection of the body, and everlasting punishment. I do not, and cannot believe in these things. And what is more, I do not want to believe in them. Father Knox does himself no good by asserting that we—for I was one of the misguided occasions of his book— 'have no stomach for the quest of Truth, which is [for us] but a series of notice-boards, announcing "No Road Here," ' and that we 'slink, baffled away.' He would like us to feel that about it, but we don't, and although I have seen Arnold Bennett, Julian Huxley, Hugh Walpole and Rebecca West, in various intellectual and social predicaments, I have never seen a less likely lot of slinkers in my life.

I have no quarrel with Father Knox's religion, so long as he does not use it to advance temporal ambitions, nor with any man's. His vision may be clear, and since at any rate he thinks it is I can even understand his pity for what he takes to be the imperfection of my own. But he must not pretend that I want his pity, or that in my heart, if I had the courage to confess it, I envy him.

That Christ was born of a virgin and that being man he was also, in a miraculous sense, God, are propositions that my mind rejects without being prepared to argue about it. As to eternal punishment for transgression, however grave, committed by a being in the imperfect conditions of time, it is a conception that can be attributed to God only in blasphemy; it is the conception of a fiend. There remains the question of revealed religion.

We are apt to be shy concerning our belief in or scepticism about God, or a god. It is a matter that may often engage two or three friends in eager debate, but they are then usually more absorbed by the debate than enlightened by its conclusions. The real problem is one that may, and frequently does, startle any one of us, suddenly, in any place or company. You may be seated with a dozen acquaintances discussing arterial roads or a general election when, without warning, all such things recede into a mist of unreality, and you perceive that you are something of which all your knowledge is indefinite, that you can explain nothing of your nature, and declare nothing of your origins and destiny. It is not a case of your foundations being shaken. You merely realise with a shock that you do not know what they are. You are yourself suddenly as remote from your own comprehension as are the enigmas of space and eternity.

Every one of us probably knows the curious sensation that Tennyson often experienced of being detached from himself, of observing himself with an intelligence that seemed to be wholly independent, and at the same time wholly baffled. We see ourselves from without, and what we see is unintelligible. This recurrent realisation comes, as I say, with a shock. But the remarkable thing is that the shock is not a shattering one; it is one that we are easily able to endure, and from which we readily recover.

That sense of bewildered isolation, so complete, as it seems, and so inescapable, might surely be expected to overwhelm us. When it is most active, I am truly conscious of one thing only, that I do not know what I am, and that all speculation beats itself in vain against that ignorance. And yet, within a few minutes, I am at ease again in my environment, aware of my natural functions, my place and responsibilities in society, my historical antecedents, and my aspirations. The ordinary vexations of life return to be met and overcome. I go about my work, slip on the frozen pavement, or observe how agreeably my orange cat shows himself off against the green grass. I am no longer in the grip of that strange immensity of fear. I have not by any conscious effort mastered it, but it has lost its control of me. How am I to account for this?

The answer, it seems to me, must be that it was not profoundly fear at all. I have been faced with something incalculable, and it is something of the most fundamental importance to me. The truth that has suddenly engaged my speculation, and has remained securely beyond my discovery, affects the whole scope of my being. In the presence of that mystery, I have no rational assurance that my life has either purpose or hope; hardly, indeed, that I am anything more than 'a tale told by an idiot, signifying nothing.' Yet I am able to emerge over and over again from this ordeal with my interests fresh and active, my mind equal to its dilemmas, and with whatever I may have of natural fortitude unimpaired.

If my rational faculties were all, this could hardly

be the case. If the enigma were really as dark as it appears to my reason, I see no means whereby I could hope to recover from the moods in which I am driven by some obscure agency to contemplate it. Madness and desolation must, it would seem, be the inevitable consequence. But they are not. And it must be because in those moods I am not merely rational in the sense that I am when in contact with the routine of daily experience. Something more than my reason comes into operation when the mystery asserts itself. That something is a belief in God.

It is useless to ask me to define what precisely is the nature of the God in whom I believe. My apprehension of him is not made by my reason, and it is by my reason alone that I am able to attempt definitions. But the fact that my conception of God is not amenable to logical terms does not make the conception itself less real or less urgent. Man, when faced with this problem, has frequently felt it necessary for his own peace to envisage his idea of God in some concrete form that could satisfy his rational senses. Zeus and Thor and Osiris and Jehovah and The Great Spirit have been mediums through which man has been able to translate his awareness of God into tangible images that he could visualise, that he could even represent in marble or wood or paint.

So personal and intimate have the images become that the distinction between one image and another has been the source of countless wars and outrages and persecutions. The images have engendered creeds, and the creeds have provoked discord. But behind the discordant creeds the images represent a concept, a belief in God, that is common to mankind. It is true that a few people profess a positive unbelief, atheism. Whether they could maintain the position under severe self-scrutiny is, at least, doubtful, and in any case the position is a rare one. Others, again, profess agnosticism; they are content to say that they do not know whether or not there is a God, and to leave it at that. Yet again, others fortify their belief in God through one of the accepted images.

There are immense numbers of people who belong to none of these categories. They believe profoundly in God, but they seek no material symbol for their faith. To them the attempt to reduce to terms of reason a revelation that they perceive by a faculty that transcends reason is one that seems purposeless. The material world, controlled by man's art into a thousand lovely and significant forms, is itself a joy to them, but a joy transfigured always to wonder. Even the material world, while they understand it sufficiently to find it admirable and delightful, is, they know, not wholly within the scope of their reason. *Macbeth*, the Pyramids, *The Magic Flute*, Salisbury Cathedral, Holbein's Duchess of

Milan, William Simmond's Black Mare—these things are sharply significant to us, and yet the significance is still but imperfectly realised by us, as indeed it must have been also by their creators.

This is true also of the natural spectacles that move us, the daily wonders of light and shade, and the growth and movement of the seasons. We catch enough of their secret to support and satisfy us; but we know that something is yet withheld. It should not trouble us. For in those moments of contact with a reality that is beyond our rational processes we know, as surely as we know anything, that there is a power through whom the full revelation will yet be made. And the power is God.

These are views that upset people like Father Knox very much indeed. I see nothing remarkable in believing in a reality that is beyond the scope of my reason. What right has Father Knox to deride me as an intellectutal sloven or half-wit for confessing that my instinct asserts this reality, while asserting also that my reason is not competent to confirm my belief? Father Knox is with me in admitting that he cannot define God or particularise God's nature, but he girds at me because I won't go beyond the assertion that I believe that there is a God by instinct to the further assertion that I know that here is a God by reason. Father Knox professes to nd in his own reason no such inadequacy. But I find in his reason a precisely similar inadequacy to my own. He falls back on revelation, and asserts that by this he knows with the full sanction of his reason. I answer that he does not know: he believes, just as I do. He may argue that his belief is supported by more tangible evidence than mine, but it happens to be evidence that impresses me less than it does him. All that it amounts to is that someone else has told him that there is a God. So great is his confidence in this assurance that he thereupon says that he knows there is a God, and that this knowledge is comprehensible to his reason. All I can say is that he must mean something by reason that I don't.

This is not to say that his evidence is, in my view, negligible. If I want to believe something, and I find that other people for whom I have respect believe it, I am comforted in my desire. I am encouraged in my own belief that there is a God by the knowledge that great numbers of good men have believed it. But nothing can induce me to say that, because they too have believed it, I know it in a manner definable by reason.

Moreover, the particular revelation that enables Father Knox to say quite confidently that, by his reason, he does know it, is involved in circumstance that for me impairs its authority, not only as establishing my reasoned knowledge but even as a support to my belief. It is inseparable from an acceptance of such supernatural phenomena as the virgin birth and the resurrection of the body. My reason, while it refrains from the attempt to follow my instinct into the region where it asserts a belief in God, is by no means antagonistic to that belief. It merely realises, without distress, that it can neither confirm nor deny the belief, however strongly it may be urged by the instinct. My reason is, indeed, braced by this communication from my instinct, but beyond that it cannot go. To these supernatural phenomena, however, my reason definitely is antagonistic. It is totally incapable of making any sense of them, or of seeing what virtue lies in their acceptance.

This is not an argument, but a confession. I have no interest whatever in persuading anybody; I wish to make my own position clear, that is all. But Father Knox's attitude towards me is quite different. He knows perfectly well that, if he had the political or temporal power, he would do one of two things to me. Either he would convert me to his way of thinking, or at least make me say that I was converted; and, failing that, he would burn me.

The revealed religion of the churches means nothing to me; nor does that other kind of revelation professed by the so-called spiritualists, who, whatever they may know of what by most of us is recognised as being unknowable, so often appear to be people of very limited intelligence on other matters about which the ordinary man can form an opinion. On the other hand, I am no more impressed by the pessimism that sees no hope or beneficent design for the individual beyond his life on earth. My unreasoned belief in God cannot conjecture a malevolent or even an indifferent presiding power. In spite of all the evil in the world there is a constant and indomitable effort towards good. Frustration everywhere is common, but fulfilment is even commoner. The physical example is not insignificant; disease abounds among us, but it is not so abundant as health. If you could strike the average condition of man's daily life, you would find a large measure of anxiety and distress, but you would find a much larger measure of faith and satisfaction. The accumulation of horrors and depravity in the world still do not set the tide flowing against good, however seriously they may impede it. And I cannot conceive of a general if slow direction towards good that does not indicate some form of personal survival. What the nature of this may be, I can no more surmise than I can define for myself the concrete nature of the God in whom I believe.

But a conception of the universe that condemns the individual life to extinction is, for me, a conception of blank despair. The individual life that does not glory in its racial authority, and proudly submit itself to the continuity that above all else invests humanity with honour, is a life of crude immaturity. Nevertheless, the doctrine that all is well with me if in a little measure I serve the race and then cease to exist, is for me a pretence that I refuse to make. If death is for anyone of us the finality, then life, in my view, is a cheat that beggars the imagination. I do not believe for an instant that death is this. I am sure that I have not at present the faculty that would enable me to realise what immortality is; but at least I have a faculty which assures me, beyond dissuasion, that immortality is the destiny of the 'quintessence of dust' which is man. I believe in God, and I cannot believe in a God who may destroy me.

In concluding, I should like for a few minutes to consider an aspect of life that in the pressing urgency of public affairs is apt to be overlooked. So much attention is necessarily paid to the public problems of conduct that beset us, that private conduct might often seem to be of relative unimportance. And yet in reality it is at the heart of the whole matter. Westminster, Washington, Paris and the rest—these are the clearing-houses of world politics, and as such they are conspicuous in a degree that is altogether disproportionate to their actual importance in our daily lives. Republican in, Liberal out; Democrat up, Tory down—what a pother is made about it all, and in reality what a little odds it all makes. When one of them effects a reform, as likely as not it is one that popular feeling dictates at the moment, and the party in power does the job, just as the other party would do it if it were in. Government has its uses, and the parties, when they do not threaten stability by caprice as they do in France, help to keep it bright and responsible. We could not do without government, but we could very well do with a little less fuss about it. In my opinion, Mr. Ramsay Mac-Donald is one of the greatest political leaders in English history, and it is, further, my good fortune to be his debtor for many personal civilities. But as I think of England while I am now with you in America, I am a great deal less interested in what is happening at Number 10 Downing Street than in what is happening at Number 9 The Grove, High-gate, where I live. And so it is with every one of us. In the sum of our lives, public affairs are but a small reckoning. The professional, domestic, social con-tacts of each individual are the elements from which any civilisation takes its tone. These contacts are worth considering.

When Cardinal Wolsey, founding Christ Church college at Oxford, gave it the celebrated motto 'Manners maketh Man,' he went straight to the mark in three words. A world of perfect manners would be a perfect world. Which means that we attribute to manners a good deal more than the conveniences of social deportment. These, indeed, are to be respected. Superficial courtesy is an admirable thing, and the people who mistake rudeness for candour are ridiculous when they are not tiresome. But genuine good manners are the product of something much profounder than the graces that we should not neglect. They are founded on the rarest of all spiritual virtues, tolerance.

By people who think loosely tolerance is often confused with indolence and timidity. They think that strength is indicated by thumping the table, preferably with a mailed fist. There are many, it seems, who have not been disillusioned even by the crude lessons of 1914. They have not learnt, probably they never will learn, that tolerance is a symptom of understanding, self-possession, power. To be tolerant is not to acquiesce weakly in the misconduct of others, nor is it to accept injustice without complaint. No one could be severer in rebuke than Christ, who nevertheless preached the doctrine of turning the other cheek. Merely to hit back in a personal quarrel is not at all the same thing as standing firmly for a principle. And the truly tolerant man knows exactly when tolerance should be exercised and when it should not.

When a man does something directly to the injury of his fellow-beings, he should be restrained. That is a broad generalisation that in practice will not be sensitive enough to determine border-line cases of conduct, but it will serve our purpose. Is a starving man, for example, who steals a loaf of bread from the rich man's table doing his fellows an injury? We need not pause to answer such a question here. The general principle holds—injury by one individual to another, or to the community, must not be tolerated. But beyond this point intolerance should not go, and this means that over by far the greater part of social behaviour tolerance should preside. The tolerant man realises that in a very small margin only of their conduct are people actually in conflict with the common good. The average citizen has no designs on the person, the property, or the legitimate interests of his fellows. And so long as he is inoffensive in these respects, the average citizen should be left alone. But there are a very great many people who dislike the idea of leaving anybody alone. By public legislation and by private criticism they are forever seeking to control and dragoon the thought and habits of other people. This is intolerance of which no defence can be made, and it is one of the most evil influences in the world. It degrades the temper of society, and does untold harm to character.

Tolerance recognises that decency is a normal

state of mind, and that differences of thought and habit, so long as they do not encroach on public liberty in its widest sense, are to be respected. The desire to regulate other people by our own tastes and opinions is an objectionable compound of fear, jealousy, and impudence. It is right for me to persuade you to my views if I can, but to penalise you if I cannot is disgraceful. Nothing is more charming in domestic life than the formative influence of one mind over another, and nothing in domestic life is more destructive than tyrannous authority in matters of taste, habit, and opinion. Beyond the family circle the same considerations apply. If I want to go to church, drink lemonade, read *The Rosary*, and practice misogyny, it is not your business to interfere with me. But neither is it my business to interfere with you if you prefer to play golf, drink ale, read *Ulysses*, and kiss the girl.

Tolerance means dignity, self-respect, humour—all the graces that make life humane and civilised. It is the source of the manners that maketh man, and there is not enough of it among us. To be intolerant is to confess a mean and trivial spirit, to become ridiculous in self-esteem—so different a thing from self-respect—and to cut adrift from the liberal pleasures of friendship and affection. It is, moreover, to contaminate all the private and public springs of conduct. If a dramatist should write a

new *Enemy of the People,* the intolerant busybody
should be his protagonist.

In conclusion let us ask, then, what are we to
make of the world as we see it to-day. I have, I
think, spoken clearly of the dangers and corruptions
among which we live, and with a due sense of their
gravity. A mood of cheerful confidence is difficult
in these days. The folly of international jealousies,
the miseries of unemployment, the anxiety that
comes of economic insecurity, and the ill effects of
high competitive pressure on the mind, weigh heav-
ily upon us. Not to be disturbed by these would re-
quire a cynicism or a dullness of comprehension
that happily are rare. We are, in fact, living in dark
times, and we may have far to go before the smother
clears away. And yet, if we can detach ourselves from
immediate misgivings and perplexities, I do not feel
that we should be dejected. On the contrary, if we
can but ensure peace in the world for ourselves and
our children, I think that our vast civilisation
may look forward to a period of intelligent prosper-
ity that will create both material and spiritual
health with what may be unexampled fertility.
Hardly anything is too much to hope of the new
ideals of education and social opportunity if they
are left in peace to emerge from the evolutionary
stage through which, with so many convulsions, they
are now passing. And if a new wisdom does come to

order the world, it will find resources ready to its use such as have never been employed before. The mechanism of society to-day is so intricate that it is daring a good deal to hope that it will presently be running with some of the precision that astonishes us in the great machines that man has made. But if this should happen, Wordsworth's 'joy in widest commonalty spread' might prove to be not so impossible an ideal after all.

The duty of every one of us is to do all we can to give the coming age a chance of realising the hope. We have not behaved ourselves very well during the past twenty years, but we can make some amends yet. And first, what we need is faith. We must believe that recovery is possible. To doubt it in thought or word or deed is to add to the burden of those who follow us. Any wide surrender to misgivings might well be to make that burden too heavy to bear. Without courage we shall not retrieve our own fortunes, but, worse than that, we shall hand on to our children a legacy of fear. That, indeed, would be a shameful thing to do, and before we who are of the war generation finish, let us at least see to it that history does not say of us that we were the men who, having endured so much, lost heart at the end.

Fortunately, the natural spirit of man is rich in stamina and resource. Even in extreme adversity man wakes up each morning with a conviction that

somehow or another all will yet be well. This may
not be true of some wretched individuals who have
been overtried by circumstance; but it is true of the
race. Robert Browning is, perhaps, a poet who is a
little out of fashion in these days, but his greatness
is not thereby diminished, and when we search down
through the ordeals and afflictions of a greatly troubled age, we find in the foundations of our lives
much still of the intrepid resolution that was his gospel. The average man to-day, beset by a thousand
devils of discord, is a queer troubled creature in his
external behaviour. But in spite of it all, the average man to-day remains one of whom it will, we believe, yet be fitting to say that he

. . . never turned his back but march'd breast forward,
    Never doubted clouds would break,
Never dream'd, though right were worsted, wrong would
    triumph,
Held we fall to rise, are baffled to fight better,
    Sleep to wake.

———o———